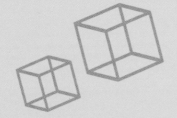

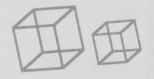

3-D Shapes

Cubes

by Nathan Olson

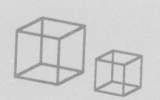

Capstone
press.

Mankato, Minnesota

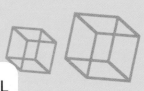

A+ Books are published by Capstone Press,
151 Good Counsel Drive, P.O. Box 669, Mankato, Minnesota 56002.
www.capstonepress.com

1 2 3 4 5 6 12 11 10 09 08 07

Library of Congress Cataloging-in-Publication Data
Olson, Nathan.
  Cubes / by Nathan Olson.
  p. cm.—(A+ books. 3-D shapes)
  Summary: "Simple text and color photographs introduce cube shapes and give examples of cubes
in the real world"—Provided by publisher.
  Includes bibliographical references and index.
  ISBN-13: 978-1-4296-0049-1 (hardcover)
  ISBN-10: 1-4296-0049-7 (hardcover)
  1. Cube—Juvenile literature. 2. Shapes—Juvenile literature. 3. Geometry, Solid—Juvenile literature.
I. Title. II. Series.
QA491.O443 2008
516'.156—dc22   2006037423

Credits

Jenny Marks, editor; Alison Thiele, designer; Scott Thoms and Charlene Deyle, photo researchers;
  Kelly Garvin, photo stylist

Photo Credits

Capstone Press/Alison Thiele, cover (illustrations), 29 (illustration); Karon Dubke, 4, 5, 6, 8–9, 10, 11,
  12–13, 14, 15, 16, 17, 18–19, 22, 23, 24–25, 26, 27, 29 (craft)
Getty Images Inc./Koichi Kamoshida, 21
Peter Arnold/Secret Sea Visions, 20

Note to Parents, Teachers, and Librarians

This 3-D Shapes book uses full color photographs and a nonfiction format to introduce the concept
of cube shapes. *Cubes* is designed to be read aloud to a pre-reader or to be read independently
by an early reader. Photographs help listeners and early readers understand the text and concepts
discussed. The book encourages further learning by including the following sections: Table of
Contents, It's a Fact, Hands On, Glossary, Read More, Internet Sites, and Index. Early readers may
need assistance using these features.

Table of Contents

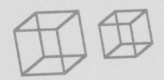

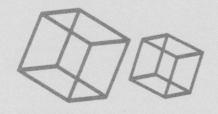

What Are 3-D Shapes?

Circles and squares are flat, or two-dimensional, shapes. 2-D shapes have height and width, but not depth.

Balls, hats, and other toys have height, width, and depth. These shapes are three-dimensional, or 3-D.

The top, bottom, and sides of a
cube are equal squares. Each side
is called a face. The side that
a cube sits on is called its base.

base

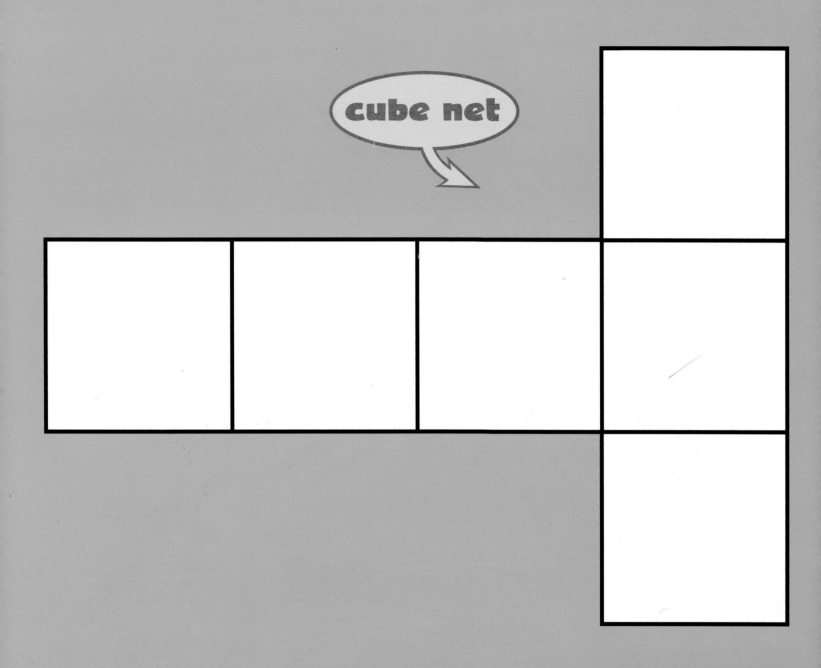

Six equal squares combine
to make the cube's net.

Playing with Cubes

A surprise pops out
of a cube called
a jack-in-the-box.

Alphabet blocks with six equal sides are cubes too.

Cubes called dice have
tiny dots on each side.

Tasting Cubes

Little grains of sugar pressed
into cubes taste like candy
to a hungry pony.

Toasted bread cubes are called croutons. They add a tasty crunch to soup.

How about some cheese, please?
Orange cubes of cheddar are
a bite-sized treat.

Creamy cubes of fancy fudge
taste oh so sweet.

Cubes of ice keep tangy lemonade nice and cold.

17

All Kinds of Cubes

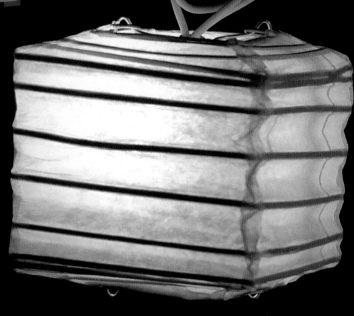

A colorful string of lantern cubes lights up the night.

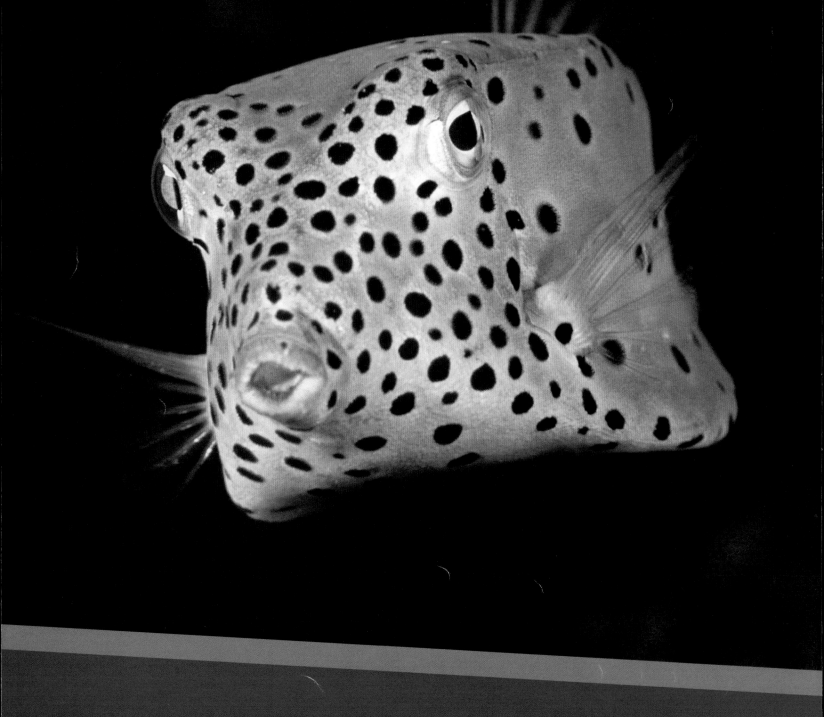

A funny little boxfish looks like
a spotted, swimming cube.

Watermelons can be grown into cube shapes. A watermelon cube won't roll off the shelf!

Cube-shaped beads spell out
names of best friends.

A giant cube lets you rest your feet while you read.

Cake cubes are good enough to eat. But sometimes the best part of a cube is what's hiding inside!

It's a Fact

How do you grow a cube-shaped watermelon? When it's tiny, you put it in a clear cube-shaped container. The melon forms to that shape as it grows.

How does a jack-in-the-box pop open? Turning the crank on the side of the box plays music, but it also opens the box's top. The toy inside is attached to a spring, so when the lid opens, the toy bounces out.

A young boxfish looks more cube-shaped than an older boxfish. As the boxfish grows, its body gets longer and more round.

The word "crouton" comes from a French word that means "crust." Croutons are usually hard and crunchy, like some bread crusts.

A Rubik's Cube is a toy puzzle made up of many little cubes of different colors. The challenge is to arrange each of the cube's six sides with the same color.

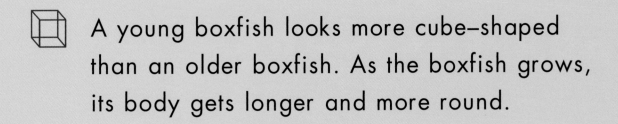

Hands On
Cubby the Cube

You can decorate a 3-D shape to make a funny friend named Cubby the Cube.

What You Need

- cube-shaped box
- glue or tape
- scissors
- assorted decorations (felt, buttons, yarn, pompons, feathers, googly eyes)

What You Do

1 Ask an adult for a cube–shaped box that you can use, like a gift box or an empty facial tissue box.

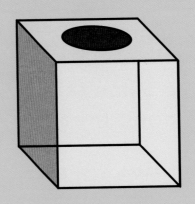

2 Glue or tape decorations on the cube to make a face for Cubby. He'll need some eyes, a nose, and a mouth. How about some wild hair? What else can you add to make Cubby look great?

Glossary

base (BAYSS)—a flat side that a 3-D shape stands on

crouton (KROO-tahn)—a small piece of crunchy dried bread

depth (DEPTH)—how deep something is

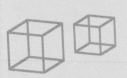

face (FAYSS)—a flat side of a 3-D shape

height (HITE)—how tall something is

three-dimensional (THREE-duh-MEN-shun-uhl)—having length, width, and height; three-dimensional is often shortened to 3-D.

two-dimensional (TOO-duh-MEN-shun-uhl)—having height and width; flat; two-dimensional is often shortened to 2-D.

width (WIDTH)—how wide something is

Read More

Kompelien, Tracy. *3-D Shapes Are Like Green Grapes! Math Made Fun.* Edina, Minn.: Abdo, 2007.

Shepard, Daniel. *Solid Shapes.* Yellow Umbrella Books for Early Readers. Bloomington, Minn.: Yellow Umbrella Books, 2006.

Internet Sites

FactHound offers a safe, fun way to find Internet sites related to this book. All of the sites on FactHound have been researched by our staff.

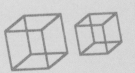

Here's how:

1. Visit *www.facthound.com*
2. Choose your grade level.
3. Type in this book ID **1429600497** for age-appropriate sites. You may also browse subjects by clicking on letters, or by clicking on pictures and words.
4. Click on the **Fetch It** button.

FactHound will fetch the best sites for you!

Index

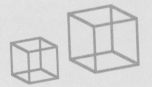